THE
Archive Photographs
SERIES

AIR TRANSPORT
THE FIRST FIFTY YEARS

THE
Archive Photographs
SERIES

AIR TRANSPORT
THE FIRST FIFTY YEARS

Compiled by
John Cook

CHALFORD

First published 1997
Copyright © John Cook, 1997

The Chalford Publishing Company
St Mary's Mill, Chalford,
Stroud, Gloucestershire, GL6 8NX

ISBN 0 7524 0790 2

Typesetting and origination by
The Chalford Publishing Company
Printed in Great Britain by
Redwood Books, Trowbridge

Contents

Acknowledgements

In these pages an attempt has been made to encapsulate fifty years of endeavour by aircraft builders, pilots, businessmen and entrepreneurs, without whom the world of commercial air transport would never have achieved the economic status that it enjoys in today's world. Their skills and determination have created an industry which is at the forefront of technology on the one hand but which, on the other, allows anyone with the fare in his or her pocket to travel to the other side of the globe as a matter of routine. All who peruse these pages owe them a debt of gratitude.

This compilation owes much to the public relations staff and photographers employed by manufacturers and airlines over the entire period and their contributions are gratefully acknowledged, though they are too numerous to list comprehensively. In particular, however, I would like to thank John Havers, Mike Hooks, Phil Jarrett, Mike Stroud and Barry Wheeler, editor of *Air Pictorial*, for delving into their archives for the more obscure items. Equally, I acknowledge the contribution of any photographer whose work has been included without my being aware of the provenance of the print being used. Finally, my thanks to the team at Chalford Publishing for the technical production of this volume and for the *Archive Photographs* concept.

Introduction

Modern air transport is mainly concerned with the transportation of people, though the underfloor freight holds of the latest wide-bodied jet airliners are able to carry substantial cargo loads and there are, of course, specialised cargo aircraft and airlines to operate them. Much of the early development of air services, however, was based on the need to improve postal communications and the aeroplane's ability to travel in relatively straight lines between the world's towns and cities, even at relatively low speed initially, made it a very promising prospect. Reliability was a problem, as was the weather, but as the decades passed technical developments came to the aid of the pilots whose responsibility it was to deliver the payload, animate or inanimate, safely to the scheduled destination. Navigation aids were non-existent, the operational range of the aircraft was relatively short and much of the terrain over which the pioneers flew was inhospitable or sparsely populated.

If these were problems in Europe, they were exaggerated in the United States. The commercial potential of aviation generated solutions and as early as the summer of 1923, the US Post Office had completed the Chicago-Cheyenne section of the 'lighted airway', providing gas-powered beacons en route and beacons, floodlights and boundary markers on terminal and emergency landing fields. Aircraft were fitted with luminous instruments, navigation lights, landing lights and carried parachute flares. These facilities allowed night flying to take place on the transcontinental mail route and reduced the coast-to-coast scheduled time to about 26 hours eastbound and 34 hours westbound.

Elsewhere, technical advances were also made, including better instrumentation, the introduction of radio, weather forecasting and more reliable engines. Improved airfield facilities were required as aircraft grew larger and heavier, necessitating the provision of concrete runways; passengers, too, demanded more than the wooden buildings that passed for terminals in the early days. In the mid 1930s high-altitude weather research was undertaken to allow commercial flights to take advantage of better conditions above the clouds but it was not until the advent of the world's first pressurised airliner, the Boeing 307 Stratoliner, that regular 'above-the weather' flights could be made.

The Second World War accelerated the development of airframes, engines and equipment, and much of the technology born of military necessity was readily transferrable to civil programmes. Equally, the 'cold war' between the contrasting ideologies of east and west provided a continuing spur to research and development. The early post-war airliners were still relatively small, in keeping with the markets they served, but as the war-ravaged economies of the world recovered and greater affluence reached a wider section of the population in the developed world, tourism very substantially raised the numbers of air travellers.

The advent of the jet engine, in particular, conferred major opportunities for the economic operation of increasingly larger aircraft with better utilisation rates than anything that had gone before. As our chosen half-century neared its end, Boeing achieved certification of the Model 747-100, an aircraft configured to carry 374 passengers in service with Pan American. Its size demanded more space on the airport ramp, more time to embark and disembark passengers, to load and unload baggage and to refuel. It marked a turning point for airport planners and brought reality to the term 'mass travel' – a far cry from the unsophisticated aircraft of 1919.

In this book, the objective has been to represent pictorially those types of aircraft that have been important to the overall story of commercial air transport, not always because they were successful. It is not an attempt to describe their technical attributes, into which readers will hopefully be inspired to research more deeply using other reference works, but to record, in an approximately chronological order, their place in the evolution of a world-shrinking and truly international industry.

One

Beginnings:
Europe and Colonial
Air Links

During the First World War, the aeroplane had progressed from the early low-powered, lightly-built observation machines to the rugged fighters and bombers which were effective weapons of war. Large quantities of surplus aircraft were available when hostilities ceased and there were trained pilots to fly them. Faster delivery of mail was the original spur but passenger services soon followed, even though there was little provision for customer comfort. Paradoxically, it was a German company, Deutsche Luft Reederei, that opened the world's first sustained daily passenger service, linking Berlin and Weimar. Although French and British companies were not far behind, the most far-reaching and comprehensive route network began to radiate from Germany. Junkers, in particular, assisted the spread of commercial aviation into Northern and Eastern Europe by setting up airlines in order to supply them with its products.

The major colonial powers wanted improved communications with their overseas possessions. France, for example, pioneered routes to North and West Africa, activity exemplified by Lignes Aériennes Latécoère, based at Toulouse. Initial flights to Barcelona were progressively extended to Alicante, then to Malaga, before the Mediterranean was crossed in an extension to Casablanca. Renamed Aéropostale in 1927, the airline began flying in South America, linking Natal with Buenos Aires via Rio de Janeiro and Montevideo, and on 12 May 1930, Jean Mermoz and his crew made a non-stop mail flight across the South Atlantic from Dakar to Natal.

The Dutch developed the route to the East Indies, opening a scheduled route from Amsterdam to Batavia on 1 October 1931 and the Belgians achieved regular service from Brussels to Leopoldville in February 1935. The British threw their energies into an earth-girdling service through the Middle East, India and the southeast corner of Asia to Australia, and to South Africa. A mail service to Cape Town was inaugurated on 20 January 1932, including rail sectors from Paris to Brindisi and from Alexandria to Cairo; passengers were carried through to the Cape from 27 April. Similarly, an air and train route from London reached Cairo in 1926, was extended to Basra in January 1927 and to Karachi in March 1929. Further sectors followed in 1933, to Calcutta, then Rangoon and to Singapore in December. The route to Brisbane and later, to Sydney, was completed in December 1934. Germany's economic and political links with South America led to the establishment of airlines in several of the countries of the southern half of the continent and to the technically demanding trial mail services across the South Atlantic.

All of this route development took place in a little under twenty years, and the need for more speed, range, reliability and capacity resulted in the appearance of a succession of new designs, each offering perfomance improvements over its predecessors. Junkers had built all-metal transport aircraft from as early as 1919, when the first F 13 made its maiden flight, and its pre-war line culminated in the 40-seat, 200 mph Ju 90. Fokker, on the other hand stuck to its wooden structures but still sold extensively to export markets as well as to domestic customer KLM. Dornier's speciality was flying boats, as was that of Short Brothers whose C-class Empire boat was Imperial Airways' standard longhaul aircraft from its introduction in 1936 until its eventual retirement, with successor BOAC, in 1947; the C-class fleet flew almost 38 million miles in that period.

Many of the other great names of aircraft manufacture made their contributions – Bleriot, Caudron, Dewoitine, Latécoère, Lioré et Olivier, Potez and Wibault from France, Blohm & Voss, Heinkel and Focke-Wulf from Germany, Macchi and Savoia Marchetti from Italy. Britain's pioneers included Armstrong Whitworth, Avro, de Havilland, Handley Page, Spartan and Westland, and in the second half of the 1930s the first US-built aircraft began to make their presence felt as imports of the Douglas DC-2 and DC-3 began to flow through the Fokker agency.

The German company Deutsche Luft Reederei began the world's first sustained domestic scheduled service on 5 February 1919, linking Berlin with Weimar via Leipzig. Left to right are a Rumpler CIV, an AEG K and a Friedrichshafen G.IIIa.

Protected from the elements by suitable flying clothing, a passenger climbs aboard a Deutsche Luft Reederei LVG CIV at Berlin's Johannisthal airfield. DLR started its second route, from Berlin to Hamburg, on 1 March 1919.

Converted Freidrichshafen G.IIIa bombers were among Deutsche Luft Reederei aircraft used in November 1919 to carry mail from Berlin to other German cities during a period of strikes and coal shortage which brought ground traffic to a halt.

SNETA's Fokker DVII O-BEBE was the first aircraft entered on the Belgian civil register when it was opened on 19 March 1919. Other SNETA aircraft in this scene at Brussels-Evère are Fokker DVII O-BILL, Rumpler CIVs O-BRUN and O-BREF, Breguet 14s O-BLOC and O-BROC, and Rumpler CIV O-BUIS.

Based on the de Havilland D.H.4 but with a modified rear fuselage to incorporate a 4-seat passenger cabin, the D.H.16, exemplified here by G-EARU, was used by Air Transport & Travel Ltd to inaugurate the world's first regular daily international passenger service, from London to Paris, on 25 August 1919. Nine were built, eight of them for AT&T.

The scene upon the arrival in Amsterdam of Air Transport & Travel's de Havilland D.H.9 G-EALU on 17 May 1920, operating the very first service of the Royal Dutch Airline KLM. The pilot for the flight from Croydon was Captain 'Jerry' Shaw, two British journalists were the passengers and a small consignment of English newspapers was carried.

Converted Breguet 14A2 reconnaissance aircraft were first used in civil guise by Lignes Aériennes Latécoère which opened a Toulouse-Barcelona mainly-mail service on 25 December 1925. Cie des Messageries Aériennes was another major user, beginning operations on 18 April 1919 with a cargo service from Paris to Lille. In August, Brussels became a new destination and London was added in September.

Developed from the First World War Spad fighters, the Berline series of passenger carrying versions included the 1920 Spad 33. The forty production aircraft included five for the Belgian airline SNETA, one of which was O-BAHE. Four passengers were seated in the cabin and a fifth beside the pilot in the side-by-side open cockpits.

Handley Page subsidiary, Handley Page Air Transport, operated nine 10/12-passenger O/10 conversions of the O/400 bomber. They entered service in July and August 1920, flying daily from Cricklewood to European destinations such as Amsterdam, Brussels and Paris. G-EATH was the last to leave service, having been based at Le Bourget Airport in Paris and used to inaugurate a service from there to Basel and Zurich in 1923. It was flown back to Croydon in 1924 and scrapped.

The First World War ended before the Farman F.50 could operate extensively in its intended role as a military bomber but it was developed as the F.60 Goliath civil transport, powered by two Salmson 9Z radial engines and carrying twelve passengers at a cruising speed of about 62 mph (100 km/h). F-FARI was operated by the manufacturer's own airline Lignes Aériennes Farman and some aircraft remained in service with Air Union as late as the early 1930s.

In the Belgian Congo the Ligne Aérienne du Roi Albert (LARA) began to exploit the communications advantages of the aeroplane as early as 1 July 1920, using 3-seat Levy Lepen seaplanes on a 350 mile route from Kinshasa to Ngombe. This was extended in 1921 to Lisala and then to Stanleyville, a total distance of almost 1,100 miles. The company ceased operations in 1922.

Two 9-passenger de Havilland D.H.34s were ordered by Daimler Hire Ltd and the first, registered G-EBBQ, flew on 26 March 1922. It flew its first service, from London to Paris, on 2 April. Twelve were eventually built, including one for the Soviet airline Dobrolet.

Deutsch-Russische Luftverkehrsgesellschaft (Deruluft) was formed on 24 November as a joint venture between Deutsche Luft Reederei and Soviet interests. On 30 April 1922 Fokker F.III RR1 became the first Deruluft aircraft to land at Moscow's Chodynka airport. RR3 inaugurated scheduled service from Konigsberg on 1 May; the route was extended to originate in Berlin on 2 May 1927.

Deutsche Luft Reederei and Lloyd Luftdienst merged on 6 February 1923 to form Deutsche Aero Lloyd. Newspapers are seen here being loaded into one of the company's Dornier Komet IIIs; on 15 April 1925, a similar aircraft made the first commercial crossing of the Central Alps, en route from Munich to Milan.

The French company Aéronavale began an Antibes-Ajaccio mail service in November 1921, using Donnet-Denhaut seaplanes and intending to extend the route to provide a link with North Africa. Twin-engined Liore et Olivier LeO H 13s, crewed by pilot and radio operator, were later substituted and carried up to four fare-paying persons when passenger services began in 1924.

Deutsche Aero Lloyd's Fokker F.III D 378 lands in 1924 in front of the premises housing the flying school of Ahrens & Schulz at Hamburg's Fuhlsbuttel airfield.

The Handley Page W8 series had its origins in the O/400 bomber. It was built in a number of versions, including the 12-passenger W8e trimotor. O-BAHG was the first British-built example, and four more were manufactured in Belgium by SABCA for Sabena, for use in the Belgian Congo. O-BAHO left Brussels on 12 February 1925 and arrived in Kinshasa on 3 April. The Kinshasa-Luebo service, for which the aircraft had been built, was opened on 25 April.

The mid '20s interior of a Sabena Handley Page W8e.

Deutsche Aero Lloyd had to face stiff competition from Junkers Luftverkehr whose practice had been to set up operating companies to fly the products of its factories. The German government, by cutting subsidies, forced a merger of the two organisations and Deutsche Luft Hansa was established on 6 January 1926. This ski-equipped Junkers F 13 was delivered to DLH during the first month of its existence.

Deutsche Aero Lloyd and Junkers Luftverkehr were both flying to London when they merged to form Deutsche Luft Hansa. DLH continued the route from Berlin to Croydon via Hannover and Amsterdam, the equipment used including the 10-passenger Rohrbach Roland. The type was still active with DLH as late as 1936. Four Rolands were supplied to Iberia and in 1927 they opened the first service between Madrid and Barcelona.

One of the first designs to be developed for Imperial Airways after its formation in April 1924 was the Armstrong Whitworth Argosy, a 20-passenger 3-engined biplane which flew its first service, from Croydon to Paris, on 5 August 1926. G-EBLF, initially painted in the royal blue livery inherited by Imperial from Instone Air Line, was the prototype and, repainted in silver and black, it launched the luxury London-Paris Silver Wing service on 1 May 1927. On 15 June 1928 it beat the *Flying Scotsman* train in a race from London to Edinburgh. Six more Argosies were built.

Sir Alan Cobham flew de Havilland D.H.50J G-EBFO to Melbourne and back, leaving from the River Medway at Rochester on 30 June 1926 and arriving back on the Thames at Westminster on 1 October. Queensland and Northern Territory Air Service (Qantas) later ordered two and built four D.H.50As and three D.H.50Js under licence in Australia. SABCA built three D.H.50As for Sabena and the Czech airline CSA bought seven built by Aero in Prague.

Qantas also used two of the ten de Havilland D.H.61 Giant Moths which were built at Stag Lane in the late 1920s. The Bristol Jupiter VI-powered prototype underwent flight trials in December 1927 and was shipped to Australia for MacRobertson Miller Aviation. Qantas flew G-AUJB *Apollo* and G-AUJC *Diana* on air mail services.

German-backed Syndikat Condor's Dornier J Wal *Atlantico* was used to operate the first revenue service ever flown in the country. On 3 February 1927, it flew from Porto Alegre via Pelotas to Rio Grande, a route flown on a scheduled basis from 22 February. Sold in June to newly-formed Brazilian airline VARIG, as P-BAAA it became the first aircraft on the Brazilian register.

An Imperial Airways requirement for five aircraft with which to operate a Cairo-Karachi desert air mail route was met by the 10-passenger de Havilland D.H.66 Hercules which went into service in January 1927. West Australian Airways bought four, one of which inaugurated a Perth-Adelaide route on 2 June 1929.

Apron scene at Amsterdam's Schiphol Airport, the assembled aircraft including AB Aerotransport's Junkers G 23 S-AAAE which opened the Malmo-Hamburg-Amsterdam service on 15 May 1925.

Approximately forty Latécoère 28s were delivered to Aéropostale, formed in 1927, as the successor to Lignes Aériennes Latécoère which had been established in 1918. Seen at Latécoère's Montaudran factory, near Toulouse, No.930 became F-AJUX of Aéropostale. Late 28 F-AJNQ was used by Jean Mermoz and his two crew members on 12/13 May 1930 to make a 21 hour South Atlantic crossing between St Louis, Senegal and Natal, Brazil, as part of the first through air mail flight from Toulouse to Rio de Janeiro.

KLM required an aircraft with greater load-carrying capability than the single-engined F.VII and Fokker developed the F.VIII, first flown on 12 March 1927, which was designed to carry fifteen passengers; the forward fuselage baggage, cargo and mail hold was loaded through the nose. Six were delivered to KLM in 1928.

Two prototypes of the Lioré et Olivier LeO 21s were built and they were introduced on Air Union's Paris-London service on 30 July 1927. The second was later configured as a 12-seat restaurant, with a bar, and operated in collaboration with Cie Wagons-Lits. Ten production LeO 213s were delivered to Air Union between 1929 and 1931, other routes for these 18-passenger airliners including Paris-Lyon-Marseille and Paris-Geneva. They passed to Air France upon the latter's formation on 30 August 1933 and replacement by Potez 62s began in 1934.

Developed from the 6-passenger Breguet 26T, the improved 28T series was used by Air Orient and Air Union before transfer to the newly-formed Air France in August 1933. Nine Renault 12Jb-engined 280Ts were built and eight 284Ts with Hispano-Suiza 12Lbrx engines, including Air Union's F-AJTF.

Bleriot began a series of civil airliners with the Type115, a 4-engined 8-passenger biplane which flew in May 1923. In July 1924 Air Union put two of the improved Bleriot 135s into service on the Paris-London route and flew two of the larger Bleriot 155s between May and October 1926. F-AITU was one of Air Union's two 16-passenger Bleriot 165s which had two 450 hp Gnome-Rhône Jupiter radials in place of the 155's four 230 hp Renault 8Fq engines.

Syndicato Condor was registered as a Brazilian company on 1 December 1927 and on 28 January 1928 was granted rights to establish routes throughout Brazil. Its early equipment included Junkers G 24 floatplane P-BAHA.

Deutsche Luft Hansa's destinations are listed on the roof of the bus collecting passengers from a Junkers G 24 at Berlin-Templehof. Passengers flew in relative comfort in the all-metal airliner but the two pilots were still exposed to the elements in open cockpits.

D-2000 was the prototype Junkers G 38a, flown for the first time on 6 November 1929. The windows in the leading edge of the wing were for passengers in the 3-seat cabins located within the wing on both sides of the aircraft; total capacity was thirty passengers, including seats in cabins on two levels within the fuselage. Delivered in June 1930 to Deutsche Luft Hansa, it was later replaced by the 34-passenger G 38ce D-2500, which was delivered on 1 September 1931 and used on various routes up to the outbreak of the Second World War, including Berlin-Hannover-London in 1932.

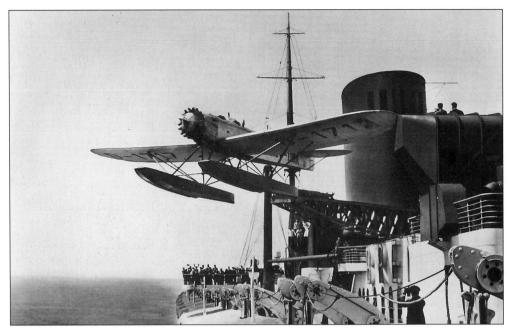

On 22 July 1929, the Heinkel He 12 D-1717 *New York* was catapulted from the Norddeutschen Lloyd Line's *Bremen*, which was on its maiden voyage, to hasten the delivery of 11,000 letters to New York. It left the ship 45 minutes flying time from port but beat the liner into harbour by five hours. The He 58 D-1919 *Atlantik*, built in 1930, was generally similar but could carry more mail.

Contemporary security personnel would look somewhat askance at the airside public refreshment facilties seen behind KLM's Fokker F.VIIb/3m PH-AEZ. This version was built under licence in Belgium, Czechoslovakia, Italy, Poland and in Great Britain. The type was used by KLM to inaugurate, on 12 September 1929, what was then the world's longest route, from Amsterdam to Batavia.

Mail delivery between Buenos Aires and Germany was hastened by two days after an initial transfer took place on 22 March 1930, near the island of Fernando de Noronha, from Dornier Wal P-BAMA *Jangadeiro* to the Hamburg Sudamerikansiche Line flagship *Cap Arcona*. Wal P-BALA *Olinda* is seen making a later rendezvous with the same vessel.

The prototype Westland Wessex G-ABAJ became OO-AGC when delivered to Sabena as part of a batch of four which were used on the Belgian airline's European routes. First flown in May 1930, the Wessex was powered by three Armstrong Siddeley Genet Major radial engines and carried two pilots and four passengers.

Junkers F 13 floatplanes, exemplified by P-BAJA *Iguasso*, played an important role in developing Brazil's early air services. When the coastal route from Rio de Janeiro north to Natal was finally inaugurated on 5 February 1930, it was an F 13 that flew the northern segment from Salvador; the segment from Rio had been operated by a Dornier Wal.

Flown in November 1930, the prototype Wibault 280 F-AKEK was re-engined and was the forerunner of the production Wibault-Penhoet 282. Six were built and one, together with the prototype, was delivered to CIDNA in 1933 for the French airline's Paris-Prague-Warsaw route. Others flew with Air Union, replacing the LeO 213 on the Paris-London route, and all passed to Air France when it was formed in August 1933. Ten 283 variants were also built for Air France in 1934; the Wibaults were replaced by the Bloch 220 in 1938.

In March 1931, KLM introduced the 16-passenger Fokker F.XII on the Amsterdam-Batavia route, replacing Fokker F.VIIb/3m aircraft. Eleven were built by Fokker, including one for AB Aerotransport of Sweden; the rest were for KLM and its East Indies subsidiary KNILM. Two more were licence-built by Orlogsvaerftet in Denmark for DDL's services from Copenhagen to Berlin, Hamburg and Hannover.

Imperial Airways ordered three Short Kent flying boats to provide non-stop capablility between Mirabella and Alexandria when the Italians closed their seaports to the British airline in October 1929 when the latter refused to pool revenues on the Genoa-Alexandria section of its route from London to Cairo. The result was the Short Kent which went into service on 16 May 1931.

First flown late in 1930, the first Savoia-Marchetti S.71 8/10-passenger trimotor I-AAYP was one of four aircraft powered by 240 hp Walter Castor radial engines, and two with 370 hp Piaggio Stella VII radials, which joined the fleet of Societa Aerea Mediterranea and which were assigned to a Rome-Brindisi service inaugurated on 6 July 1931. The company was absorbed into Ala Littoria in October 1934 and the S.71s' activities included operation of a Rome-Salonika route.

In the early 1930s A.V. Roe & Co Ltd built fourteen examples of the Fokker F.VIIB/3m as the Avro Ten – for eight passengers and a crew of two. VH-UNJ was one of two originally delivered to Queensland Air Navigation Ltd and was taken over by New England Airways Ltd to fly the Brisbane-Narrowmine section of the Empire air mail route.

The Polish airline Polskie Linje Lotnicze (LOT), formed on 1 January 1929, opened a Warsaw-Bucharest service in 1931 and close inspection of the original print of ski-equipped Fokker F.VIIb/3m SP-ABC reveals a placard beneath the cabin windows which records the use of this aircraft on the route.

Breguet flew the prototype Type 39 sesquiplane in January 1931 and supplied six examples of the production Bre 393T to Air France. With seats for ten passengers, the Bre 393T was powered by three 350 hp Gnome-Rhône radial engines.

Handley Page H.P.42E G-AAGX *Hannibal* began flying Imperial Airways' London-Paris route on 11 June 1931. G-AAXF *Helena* was the third of four 32-passenger H.P.42Ws built for European routes and, on 20 January 1932, it flew the London-Paris sector of the first through air mail service to Cape Town. Four 14/24-seat H.P.42Es were also delivered for use on services from Cairo to Kisumu and to Karachi and Delhi.

Eight Armstrong Whitworth Atlantas were built in 1931-32 for Imperial Airways, for use on the Nairobi-Cape Town and Karachi-Singapore sectors of the company's Empire air mail routes to South Africa and Australia, respectively. Behind the forward freight and mail compartment was a spacious cabin for nine passengers. Three were lost in crashes, including G-ABTG at Kisumu, Kenya on 27 July 1938, but the surviving five were used by Imperial Airways and subsidiary Indian Trans-Continental Airways until transferred to the Indian Air Force in March 1941.

Two bright red Junkers Ju 46fi mailplanes extended the concept of mail delivery from ships at sea. Built in 1932, D-2244 *Europa* and D-2271 *Bremen* were catapult-launched from the liners whose names they bore, flying 750 miles to shore and arriving 24 hours ahead of their respective parent ship.

CH-167 was the first of two Lockheed Orions bought by Swissair. Fast and comfortable, with seats for six passengers, they were introduced on services linking Zurich with Munich and Vienna in May 1932. They were sold in 1936, via French agents, to form part of the transport resource available to the Republican side in the Spanish Civil War.

In addition to the two shipboard mailplanes which operated from the liners *Bremen* and *Europa*, Junkers built two landplane freighters which were delivered to Deutsche Lufthansa in 1933. D-OBRA, at least, was later float-equipped for use on the airline's holiday services to the North Sea and Baltic Sea resorts.

de Havilland's D.H.84 Dragon was developed to meet a Hillman's Airways requirement for a six-passenger, twin-engined aircraft for use on its new Romford-Paris service which opened on 1 April 1933. EI-ABI *Iolar* was the first aircraft operated by the Irish airline Aer Lingus.

Spartan Aircraft built the Cruiser tri-motors in its factory at East Cowes, Isle of Wight. The Cruiser III could carry eight passengers in addition to the crew of two and was used by Spartan Air Lines Ltd which had begun a Heston-Cowes route on 1 April 1933. British Airways absorbed the company in 1936 and moved the Cruisers to Southampton-Eastleigh to operate a Cowes, Heston, Blackpool and Isle of Man network. They later flew 'highlands and islands' services with Scottish Airways until 1940.

When Deutsche Lufthansa inaugurated the first regular trans-Atlantic mail service on 3 February 1934, mail was carried from Stuttgart to Seville in a Heinkel He 70 and then in a Junkers Ju 52/3m to Bathhurst. A Dornier Wal flying boat was used to fly the sector to Natal, Brazil and made use of the depot ship *Westfalen* which was located in the mid-Atlantic. The Wal was winched aboard for refuelling and maintenance and then relaunched by catapult. The mail completed its journey to Buenos Aires in a Junkers W 34 of Syndicato Condor.

Qantas was responsible for the Singapore-Brisbane section of the Empire air mail route to Australia, inaugurated as a through service on 8 December 1934. The airline sponsored development of the de Havilland D.H.86 and bought 6. The prototype was G-ACPL, flown on 14 January 1934, which differed from production aircraft in that it had a single-pilot cockpit. The Australian authorities required 2 pilots and the D.H.86 also carried a radio operator, in addition to 10 passengers.

A landplane version of the Kent flying boat, the Short L.17, used the same wings and tail unit as the earlier aircraft fitted to a new fuselage which was configured in 3 cabins for 29 passengers. Two were built and were initially assigned to the Croydon-Paris route, starting in June 1934.

Four Piaggio Stella XR radial engines powered the Savoia Marchetti S.74. A small number of the 20/27-passenger airliners entered service with Ala Littoria in the mid 1930s.

The prototype Potez 62 F-ANPG shows off its aerofoil section fuselage. Flown for the first time on 28 January 1935, it featured retractable landing gear and its two spacious cabins seated 6 and 8 passengers, respectively. It and 11 production Potez 62-0s were delivered to Air France that year and were assigned to services from Paris to Madrid, Marseille and Rome. Eleven Potez 62-1s were also acquired and use was extended to routes to the Far East and the trans-Andes Buenos Aires-Santiago service.

The Gipsy Six engines developed for the D.H.86 were selected for an improved Dragon, flown on 17 April 1934 and initially known as the D.H.89 Dragon Six. A 6/8-seater, the renamed Dragon Rapide quickly found favour with scheduled, charter and air taxi operators in the UK and abroad, and initial deliveries included seven for Hillman's Airways. The Olley Air Service Rapide G-ACYR was used to fly General Franco from Las Palmas to Spanish Morocco at the beginning of the Spanish Civil War. It survives in the Museo del Aire in Madrid.

An early example of mixed-class passenger accommodation was the Breguet 530 Saigon, the civil version of the Bre. 521 Bizerte long-range reconnaissance flying boat which was itself based on the Short Calcutta for which Breguet had obtained a licence. Two Saigons were built, each with 3 cabins to accommodate 3 de-luxe class, 6 first class and 11 second class passengers. They entered service early in 1935 on the Air France route from Marseille to Ajaccio and Tunis.

Following the maiden flight of the prototype Bloch 220 in December 1935, 16 production aircraft were built for Air France to replace Potez 62s and Wibault 282s on the company's main European routes. They were introduced on the Paris-Marseilles services late in 1937 and began Paris-London operations on 27 March 1938. Front and rear cabins seated 6 and 10 passengers, respectively. F-AOHD *Auvergne* was the third production Bloch 220.

Ala Littoria was the sole customer for the Macchi MC.94 12-passenger amphibian which flew for the first time in 1935. On the protoype I-NEPI, the wheels retracted forward and upward into streamlined recesses in the wing leading edges. Twelve production MC.94s were built, deliveries beginning in 1936; they were used on Northern Adriatic routes and that from Brindisi to Haifa via Athens and Rhodes.

The Caudron C.440 Goeland appeared in 1935 and was to remain in production throughout the Second World War and after hostilities ceased, total production amounting to 1,702 aircraft. Pre-war it was used as a 6-passenger light transport by Air Bleu, Air Afrique and Air France. Air Bleu Goelands began the first night postal flights on 10 May 1939, linking Paris, Bordeaux and Pau.

Air France numbered 29 Dewoitine 338s in its pre-war fleet. Seating 22 passengers, they entered service on the Paris-Cannes route in mid-1936 and were later operated on the Paris-Dakar service. Seats were reduced to 15/18 on medium-range routes and 6, plus 6 sleeping berths, on those such as Damascus-Hanoi, introduced early in 1938 and extended to Hong Kong on 10 August. From 16 March 1939 D.338s flew the Natal-Buenos Aires section of the Air France South Atlantic route.

Designed for use both as an airliner and a bomber, the 10-passenger Junkers Ju 86 was used by Deutsche Lufthansa from 1936 until 1940, mainly on internal routes. Swissair began operating HB-IXI on its Zurich-Frankfurt night mail service in April 1936. Of rather more than 60 civil Ju 86s which were built, South African Airways bought 17 Pratt & Whitney Hornet-engined Ju-86Zs and 1 Ju-86K. Deliveries began in June 1937 and the aircraft were transferred to the South African Air Force in 1939.

Fritz W. Hammer, one of the original founders of Syndikat Condor, founded Sociedad Ecuatoriana de Transportes Aereos (SEDTA) on 24 July 1937. Deutsche Lufthansa (DLH) was the majority shareholder and the company's equipment included Junkers Ju 52/3m HC-SAC *Guayas*, which had earlier flown with Syndicato Condor as PP-CBR and, before that, with DLH as D-AQUQ.

The prototype 26-passenger Lioré et Olivier H-246 flying boat F-AOUJ flew for the first time on 30 September 1937 and, in January 1938, Air France ordered six production examples for use on its Marignane-Algiers route. From October 1939 to November 1942, H-246s flew this route under the Vichy regime but they were then seized by the Luftwaffe for use as armed troop carriers. Two survived hostilities to fly again on the Algiers service until withdrawn in 1947.

Two de Havilland D.H.91 Albatrosses were originally built as mailplanes, to carry a 1,000 lb payload non-stop from Britain to North America; the first of these was flown on 20 May 1937. Imperial Airways ordered 5, configured for 22 passengers, which began operating services in January 1939 from London to Paris, Brussels and Zurich. They became part of the BOAC fleet when that airline was formed in April 1940 and flew wartime services to Lisbon and Shannon – the survivors were scrapped in 1943.

Forty-six Douglas DC-3s, sold in Europe through Fokker before the start of the Second World War, included Ceskoslovenka Letecka Spolecnost's OK-AIE which is seen about to depart from Croydon.

Anthony Fokker acquired the European sales and licence production rights for both the Lockheed 10A Electra, exemplified by British Airways' G-AESY, and the Douglas DC-2. The Lockheed deal was cancelled in 1936 but Fokker sold thirty-nine DC-2s in Europe, customers including KLM, of course.

For its planned North Atlantic mail services, Deutsche Lufthansa specified a floatplane capable of carrying a 1,102 lb (500 kg) for at least 3,106 miles (5,000 km) at a cruising speed of 155.3 mph (250 km/h). Two examples of the resulting Blohm and Voss Ha 139 began trial flights between the Azores and New York on 15 August 1937, using the depot ships *Freisenland* and *Schwabenland*. Three Ha 139s entered regular South Atlantic service in October 1938.

Imperial Airways ordered 28 Short S.23 Empire flying boats straight from the drawing board. The C-class boats were designed to carry 3,360 lb (1,524 kg) of mail and 24 day passengers, with an alternative 16 sleeping berth configuration. From 4 February 1937 they replaced the variety of types flying the overland route to Australia. Through services from Hythe to Durban began on 28 June 1937.

Sabena had bought a fleet of twelve 14-passenger Savoia-Marchetti S.73s in 1935, including seven built under licence by SABCA, and introduced the more advanced SM.83 in 1938 – three are pictured at Evère, Brussels. Bruno Mussolini's Linee Aeree Transcontinentali Italiane used the SM.83 to launch a Rome-Rio de Janeiro service in December 1939, flying via Seville, Rio de Oro, Cape Verde Islands, Natal and Recife. This closed on 11 December 1941 when fuel supplies were withdrawn at the western end of the route because of Allied pressure.

D-AGNT was the prototype Dornier Do 26, flown on 21 May 1938. The rear pair of the four tandem mounted Junkers Jumo 205 diesel engines could be tilted upwards by 10 degrees to be clear of take-off spray. Designed for Deutsche Lufthansa to carry mail non-stop across the North Atlantic from Lisbon to New York, it and the second prototype D-AWDS made just eighteen crossings over the South Atlantic before war brought flights to a premature end.

Deutsche Lufthansa was the only customer for the Junkers Ju 90, ultimately taking delivery of 11 examples of this development of the Ju 89 bomber. Normally seating 40 passengers in a cabin which could be divided into up to 5 sections, each with 4 pairs of seats in facing rows, the Ju 90 entered service in 1938 on the Berlin-Vienna route. D-AURE, powered by the BMW 132 H engines specified for the production B-series, was the third prototype.

Although an order for 12 Armstrong Whitworth Ensigns was placed by Imperial Airways in 1935, and later increased to 14 aircraft, the prototype G-ADSR did not fly until 24 January 1938. It was furnished with 27 seats, arranged in 3 cabins, and was configured for use on the Empire routes; some were completed as 40-seaters for European services. When war broke out, National Air Communications used Ensigns to fly food and ammunition to France and later, transferred to Cairo, they flew the Cairo-Calcutta sector of the route to Australia until retired in 1945.

Focke-Wulf flew the prototype Fw 200 Condor on 27 July 1937. Later re-designated Fw 200S-1, on 10 August it flew non-stop from Berlin to New York in 24 hours 56 minutes, returning on 13 August in 19 hours 55 minutes. On 28 November it flew to Tokyo via Basra, Karachi and Hanoi in 46 hours 18 minutes. Of later production examples, some were used by Lufthansa on major European services, two were sold to Denmark's DDL and two to Lufthansa's Brazilian associate Syndicato Condor.

Imperial Airways required an enlarged version of the Empire flying boat to carry mail or passengers across the North Atlantic non-stop from Foynes in Ireland to Botwood in Newfoundland, Canada. The result was the S.26 G-class, of which G-AFCI was the first of three and which flew at Rochester on 21 July 1939. War intervened before the G-Boats could be used but, after a period of armed military service, two began priority mail and passenger services from Poole to West Africa in July 1942 and in November 1944 from Kisumu to Ceylon.

PP-CBI, seen at Rio de Janeiro's Santos Dumont Airport, was one of Syndicato Condor's pair of Focke-Wulf Fw 200 Condors, delivered in 1939. With transoceanic capability, they would have been used to cross the South Atlantic on a scheduled service to Germany had war not intervened. They remained in service with the company, which was renamed Cruzeiro do Sul on 16 January 1943, until 1947 although they had been re-engined with Pratt & Whitney engines when spares for the original BMW engines became impossible to obtain because of the hostilities.

Two

US Domestic Routes and Overseas Ambitions

Although a handful of entrepreneurs had operated short-lived services over mainly short local routes from as early as January 1914, it was not until October 1925 that the US Post Office began to award commercial contracts for the carriage of mail by air, effectively giving birth to the airline industry in the United States. First to fly official mail services, on 15 February 1926, was the Ford Motor Company, operating from Detroit. Hitherto, the Post Office had been flying a substantial number of de Havilland D.H.4Bs but the advent of the commercial operators, many of them associated with the early aircraft manufacturers, quickly led to the introduction of a variety of new single-engined types, often built in small numbers.

The race was also on to provide transcontinental passenger services, initially including some rail travel. The Universal Aviation Corporation inaugurated the first such service on 14 June 1929, linking New York and Los Angeles. Passengers took the New York Central Railroad as far as Cleveland and Universal's Fokker F-XAs carried them via Chicago, St Louis and Kansas City to Garden City, Kansas where they resumed the train journey, taking the Atchison, Topeka, and Santa Fe Railroad to the West Coast. Transcontinental & Western Air began an all-air service on 25 October 1930, flown with Ford Tri-Motors and taking thirty-six hours coast-to coast, including an overnight stop at Kansas City. The southern transcontinental route, from Atlanta to Los Angeles via Dallas, had been inaugurated by American Airways on 15 October.

The first eighteen months of the 1930s was a period of merger and amalgamation. During it, the 'Big Four' of the US airline business were created – Eastern Air Transport on 17 January 1930, American Airways on 25 January, Transcontinental & Western Air on 25 October and United Air Lines on 1 July 1931. With Pan American Airways, whose pre-war activities were primarily concerned with international services, these companies were destined to dominate the industry for more than fifty years.

New airliners such as the Douglas DC-2 and the Boeing 247 were developed for Transcontinental & Western Air and United Air Lines, respectively, and Pan American's Central and South American ambitions gave birth to the big Sikorsky flying boats. The conquest of the Pacific and the Atlantic necessitated the evolution of the Boeing 314 and the Martin 130.

Technically outside the scope of this book but important as the aircraft which flew the world's first scheduled air route, the St Petersburg-Tampa Airboat Line's Benoist Type XIV took off from St Petersburg at 10.00 am on 1 January 1914, flown by Tony Jannus and carrying passenger A.C. Pheil, for a 23 minute, 18 mile flight across Tampa Bay. The alternative was a 2 hour boat trip, 12 hours on the train or almost a day by road. The service lasted 3 months and safely carried 1,204 passengers.

Aeromarine Plane and Motor Corporation's business included the conversion of surplus US Navy Curtiss flying boats for civil use and it established subsidiary Aeromarine Airways with its own products. The Type 75 was a Curtiss F-5L conversion with up to 14 seats which, late in September 1921, began the High Ball Express New York-Havana service which took 2 days, with 4 intermediate stops. Passengers were mostly circumventing the US prohibition laws. This was the prime purpose of the Miami-Bimini-Nassau flights which began in November 1921.

Edward Hubbard (left) with William E. Boeing in front of the Boeing C-700 in which they made a Vancouver-Seattle mail survey flight on 3 March 1919. This became a regular air mail service on 15 October 1920, flown by a Boeing B-1 seaplane.

Pacific Air Transport inaugurated a Los Angeles-Seattle passenger and mail service on 15 September 1926, using Ryan M-1s, of which it had ordered ten. The same aircraft was flown by Colorado Airways on its air mail service, a spur from the transcontinental route at Cheyenne which served Denver, Colorado Springs and Pueblo. The latter contract was taken over by Western Air Express on 10 December 1927.

The Curtiss Model 40 Carrier Pigeon was built for the 1925 US Post Office mailplane competition, the Liberty engine being specified. This led to an order for ten from National Air Transport when privatisation of the air mail service began in 1926. Three examples of the Carrier Pigeon II were supplied to NAT in 1929, powered by Conqueror engines which were water cooled. Note the radiator and the wing-mounted landing lights.

The Fokker Atlantic Corporation of America sold the Wright Whirlwind-powered Universal in some numbers in the late 1920s. Vern C. Gorst's Pacific Air Transport launched an all-mail service from Los Angeles to Seattle on 15 September 1926 with 2-seat Ryan M-1s but introduced the 4-seat Universal when passenger flights commenced.

One of the earliest contract mail carriers was Western Air Express, progenitor of both TWA and Western Airlines. It began operations on 17 April 1926, over contract air mail route CAM-4 which linked Salt Lake City with Los Angeles. Six Douglas M-2 single-seat mailplanes were acquired for this service.

On 1 May 1928 Pitcairn Aviation began operation of contract air mail route CAM 19, from New York to Atlanta, and used a fleet of eight of its own PA-5 Mailwings. The Atlanta-Miami contract was taken over on 1 December, giving Pitcairn a through route from the northeast to Florida. On 17 January 1930 the company's name was changed to Eastern Air Transport, forerunner of Eastern Air Lines.

Developed from the single-engined 2-AT, the Ford 4-AT Tri-Motor first entered service on 2 August 1926, with Stout Air Services on the mail contract route from Detroit to Grand Rapids. NC9685 was one of the later 5-ATs, used by Pan American Airways and its associates Compania Mexicana de Aviacion and PANAGRA.

The Boeing 40A was developed for Boeing Air Transport for use on the Chicago-San Francisco (CAM-18) section of the transcontinental mail contract route. The first aircraft flew on 20 May 1927 and all twenty-four of the aircraft required for the service had been completed and positioned along the route by the start of service on 1 July!

Dutch manufacturer Fokker's F.VIIA/3m tri-motors were used by a number of pioneering US airlines. Pan American employed the type on its Key West (later Miami)–Havana (FAM-4) Cuban mail service which was inaugurated on 19 October 1927.

Including the prototype, which flew on 4 July 1927, Lockheed built 129 Vegas, plus one which was converted from the first Model 3 Air Express. They found favour with numerous private owners but also served with early US airlines and operators in Canada and Mexico. NC7954 was used on routes between Los Angeles and Reno and from Reno to Las Vegas by Nevada Airlines in 1929-30 and was often flown by operations manager Roscoe Turner, already a keen participant in the National Air Races.

Sikorsky S-38 amphibians were chosen by Pan American Airways to develop its services throughout the islands and the countries bordering the Caribbean and the Gulf of Mexico. The S-38 went into service on 31 October 1928 and production eventually totalled 115 aircraft.

On 30 October 1928, Boeing Air Transport introduced the 14-passenger Boeing 80A on the Chicago-San Francisco (CAM-18) route. Eleven examples of the Pratt & Whitney Hornet-powered tri-motor were built.

Interstate Airlines was the customer behind the development of the Stearman LT-1 which entered service on the airline's Chicago-Atlanta air mail route CAM 30 on 1 December 1928. The company flew three of the aircraft and at least one, NC8832, was later used by American Airways.

In 1923 Pacific Marine Airlines had started a ferry service linking Wilmington, near Long Beach, California to Avalon on Catalina Island. Curtiss HS-2L flying boats were originally used but after Western Air Express had acquired Pacific Marine in June 1928, two Loening C-2H amphibians were substituted.

Western Air Express merged with Transcontinental Air Transport on 24 July 1930 to form Transcontinental and Western Air Inc. WAE continued to operate as an autonomous unit, retaining the Salt Lake City-Los Angeles (CAM-4) contract and the Cheyenne-Denver-Colorado Springs-Pueblo (CAM-12) contract. The fleet included a number of Stearman 4-DM Junior Speedmails.

The American Fokker Corporation built a number of designs for US customers, including the Fokker F-14, a parasol wing 8-passenger monoplane with which Western Air Express began services on 12 December 1929. Thirty-five were built, including C-14 cargo carriers and C-15 ambulance aircraft for the US Army.

Pan American Airways inherited the fourteen Consolidated Commodores built for the New York, Rio and Buenos Aires Line when the latter was taken over by the Aviation Corporation of the Americas on 15 September 1930. NYRBA had begun a multi-stop through-plane service from Miami to Santiago on 18 February 1930, routing through Cuba, the island chains of the Caribbean and along the east coast of South America to Montevideo, Rio de Janeiro and Buenos Aires before crossing the Andes to the Chilean capital.

Essentially a scaled-up Fokker F-X, the F-32 was, at the time, the world's largest landplane transport aircraft. It was able to carry 32 passengers by day and 16 in sleeping berths by night. Western Air Express bought 2, which carried license numbers NC333N and NC334N, and began services on 1 April 1930. Ten were built but the F-32 was prone to engine failures, mainly due to cooling problems for the rear engine of each pair of tandem-mounted Pratt & Whitney Hornet radials.

First flown on 6 May 1930, the Boeing 200 Monomail was an advanced design in which the manufacturer introduced the smooth-skinned, all-metal cantilever wing structure, with semi-retractable landing gear which it was to use later in the Model 247 airliner.

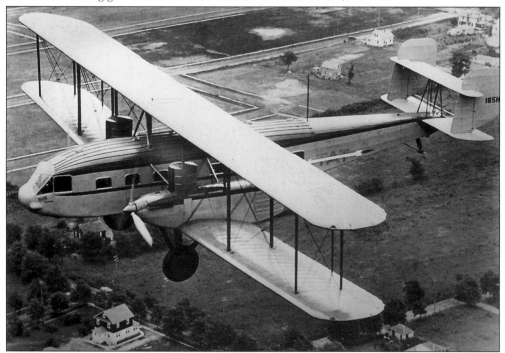

Six Model 18 Condor 18-passenger biplanes were built by the Curtiss Aeroplane & Motor Co at Garden City, New York and the type entered service with Eastern Air Transport on 10 December 1930, operating in a 12-passenger layout. NC185H, seen in Transcontinental Air Transport livery, was the first example.

Developed from the Fairchild 100, the Pilgrim 100A appeared in 1931; sixteen of these Pratt & Whitney Hornet-powered 8-passenger aircraft were supplied to American Airways. They were among successor American Airlines' disposals in mid-1934.

American Airways was established on 25 January 1930 to bring together all of the operating companies controlled by The Aviation Corporation, notably Colonial Airways Corporation, Southern Air Transport, Universal Aviation Corporation and Interstate Airways. Among the aircraft which passed to the merged airline was Fokker Super Universal NC-9129 of Universal Aviation.

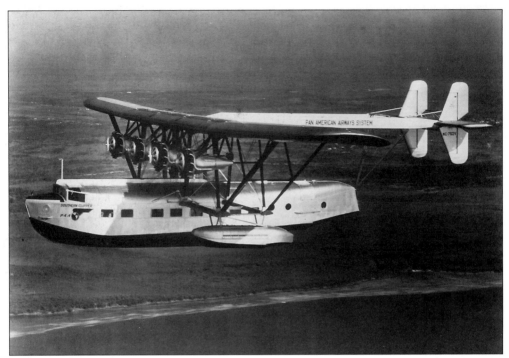

The twin boom and planing hull pod layout of the Sikorsky S-38 was adopted for the much larger 4-engined S-40 which was operated by a crew of 6 and carried 40 passengers. Three were ordered by Pan American Airways on 20 December 1929 and the first, captained by Charles Lindbergh, left Miami for the Panama Canal Zone on 19 November 1931.

Transcontinental & Western Air was the major user of Jack Northrop's Alpha mailplanes. NC924Y was one of six Alpha 3s, this being a mixed configuration model which could carry three passengers and 465 lb (211 kg) of mail. The Alpha entered service in 1931.

Seven Consolidated Model 20-A Fleetsters were built in 1932 for Transcontinental & Western Air and they entered service in October 1932 on a Detroit-Toledo-Fort Wayne-Indianapolis service which connected with the transcontinental trunk route.

NX13301 was the prototype Boeing 247, the first of the 'modern' retractable gear all-metal airliners. It flew for the first time on 8 February 1933 and the type was in service with United Air Lines as quickly as 30 March, the airline's fleet having increased to 30 by the end of June. A coast-to coast record scheduled time of 19 hours 45 minutes was established by NC13308 on 1 June 1933, beating TWA's 26 hours 45 minutes with the Ford Tri-motor.

In order to overcome inadequate take-off performance at some of the high-altitude airfields in the Rockies, the engines of the Boeing 247 were fitted with variable-pitch propellers developed by Hamilton-Standard. In this form it became the Boeing 247D. NC13315 was built for United Air Lines but was sold to Western Air Express on 12 April 1935.

Gerald Vultee designed the Vultee V-1 under the auspices of the Airplane Development Corporation, established at the Grand Central Air Terminal at Glendale, California in June 1932. The protoype X12293 flew on 19 February 1933 and 27 were built, including 20 for American Airlines. The latter put the 8-passenger V-1A production version into service on the Fort Worth-Chicago route on 9 September 1934.

Outside the Grand Central Air Terminal at Glendale, California is the unique Douglas DC-1 NX223Y, the first of the line of Douglas Commercial transports. On 19 February 1934 it set a new transcontinental record time between Los Angeles and Newark of 13 hours 4 minutes.

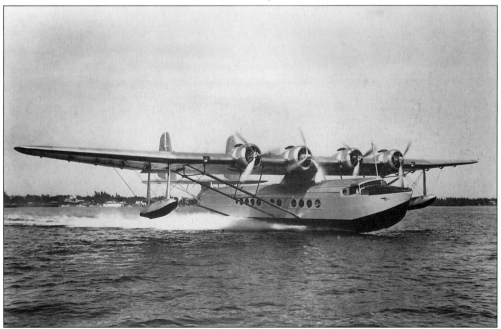

Even more advanced than the Sikorsky S-40 was the Sikorsky S-42 which weighed in at more than 20 tons (20320 kg) and could carry its thirty-two passengers plus baggage and freight for an impressive distance (then) of 750 miles (1207 km). It entered service on the Miami-Rio de Janeiro route on 16 August 1934.

American Airlines was among the operators of the Stinson Model A tri-motor, though the first to fly it, in mid-1934, was Delta Air Corporation, on its Dallas-Atlanta-Charleston air mail route. Sole export customer was Airlines of Australia which bought three in 1936 for its Sydney-Brisbane route.

TWA decided not to order the DC-1 but contracted instead to buy the larger 14-passenger DC-2. NC13711 *City of Chicago* was the first of an initial order for twenty and it began flying the Columbus-Pittsburgh-Newark route on 18 May 1934. Transcontinental services began on 1 August.

NC14716 *China Clipper* was the first of three Martin M-130 flying boats built for Pan American Airways. Under the command of Captain Ed Musick, it inaugurated the first trans-Pacific scheduled air mail route, from San Francisco to Manila, on 22 November 1935.

The slit windows in the roof of NC18101 identify it as a Douglas DST (Douglas Sleeper Transport), configured for fourteen passengers in sleeping berths. American Airlines inaugurated a transcontinental sleeper service on 18 September 1936. The shield on the nose of the Western Air Express aircraft proclaims its use on the 'Boulder Dam Route'.

Lockheed twins formed the early equipment of Trans-Canada Airlines which began revenue operations on 1 September 1937 when a Model 10A Electra, similar to CF-AZY, flew from Vancouver to Seattle. Two Model 14 H2s, exemplified by CF-TCM, took off simultaneously from Vancouver and Montreal on 1 April 1939 on the first transcontinental scheduled flights carrying fare-paying passengers.

Pan American ordered six Boeing 314s on 21 July 1936. At 82,500 lb (37422 kg), the aircraft was at that time the world's largest and most luxurious flying boat and could carry up to seventy-four passengers on short sectors. The first was delivered on 27 January 1939 and went into trans-Pacific service. NC18605 opened the world's first trans-Atlantic passenger service, from Port Washington via the Azores and Lisbon to Marseille. Pictured is Boeing 314A NC18609 in US Navy camouflage but operated by Pan American on its wartime services.

Developed from the Lockheed Super 14, the Model 18 Lodestar was flown in prototype form on 21 September 1939 and production aircraft entered service with Mid-Continent Airlines in March 1940. NC25638 was used by Western Airlines, successor to Western Air Express, on a demanding wartime service from Great Falls, Montana via Edmonton, Alberta to Fairbanks and Nome, Alaska.

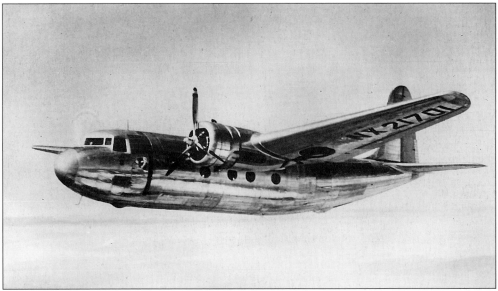

A Douglas design which achieved uncharacteristically limited success was the 16/22-seat DC-5, four of which were ordered by KLM for use in the Dutch East Indies and the Dutch West Indies. Although Pennsylvania Central Airways and the Colombian airline SCADTA ordered six and two, respectively, these were not delivered and three R3D-1 and four R3D-2 transports were built for the US Navy. NX21701 was the prototype, flown by Carl Cover at Los Angeles on 20 February 1939.

TWA introduced the Boeing 307 Stratoliner, the world's first pressurised passenger transport aircraft, on its transcontinental routes on 8 July 1940. Carrying thirty-three passengers, it reduced the coast-to-coast scheduled time to 13 hours 40 minutes. Pan American ordered three on 15 March 1937, intending to use them for experimental flights across the North Atlantic to London.

Pan American Airways ordered the Sikorsky S-43 Baby Clipper to replace its Consolidated Commodores on coastal services to South America and in the Caribbean. The S-43 went into service in April 1943.

Three

Swords into Ploughshares – Post-War Pistons

The Second World War had resulted in the virtual elimination of transport aircraft development and production outside the United States. Britain had agreed to concentrate its wartime production resources on combat aircraft and trainers and although the French, primarily in the area controlled by the Vichy regime, had continued work on some prewar projects, such as the Bloch 161 and the Latécoère 631, little real progress was made until after the cessation of hostilities when the former Axis powers, with the exception of Italy, were precluded from undertaking such activity.

In Britain, the Brabazon Committee evolved a number of specifications for aircraft in a range of categories, from eight seats upwards, and new designs began to appear in 1945. However, the immediate needs were met by converting Avro Lancaster and Handley Page Halifax bombers and Short Sunderland flying boats for civilian use. Charter and air taxi companies were largely equipped with demobilised Airspeed Oxfords, Avro Ansons and de Havilland Dominies until the US government began to make available surplus Douglas C-47 Dakotas, which had been originally supplied to the Royal Air Force under the Lease-Lend agreement .

Elsewhere in Europe, converted Douglas C-54s were used by most of the major national flag-carriers to restart international services, pending delivery of new Douglas DC-6s and Lockheed Constellations. The US had also reduced its commercial air fleet to a minimum during the war and the same ex-military equipment, including Curtiss C-46s, was made available to domestic and international airlines to begin the rebuilding of their fleets. Douglas and Lockheed, however, continued development of the DC-6 and Constellation, both culminating in the mid 1950s in larger, faster versions with powerful Wright Turbo Compound engines.

Lockheed designed the Constellation to meet a TWA specification but war intervened and the project was taken over by the USAAF as the C-69. Nevertheless, the second prototype 43-10310 was flown by TWA's Jack Frye and Howard Hughes, officially on its delivery flight, from Burbank to Washington, DC on 17 April 1944 in a record time of 6 hours, 57 minutes and 51 seconds, an average speed of 330.17 mph.

Military surplus Douglas C-54 and R5D Skymasters were sold to US airlines which were rebuilding after the Second World War. NX45341, after civil conversion by Douglas at El Segundo, was delivered to Trans World Airline on 11 March 1946 and surveyed TWA's new international routes as far as Cairo, outbound via Newfoundland, Labrador, Foynes in Ireland, Paris, Geneva, Rome, Naples and Athens. Return to Washington was via Benghazi, Tripoli, Tunis, Algiers, Casablanca, Lisbon, Newfoundland and the Azores.

Avro 691 Lancastrians were jointly operated by British Overseas Airways Corporation and Qantas on the Kangaroo route to Sydney, Australian crews taking over at Karachi. The inaugural service left Hurn, then London's long haul airport, on 31 May 1945. G-AKPZ was one of a small number of RAF Lancastrian C.2 conversions which BOAC used in 1948 to overcome capacity deficiencies resulting from late delivery of Avro Tudors.

The Avro 685 York military transport used the same wings, engines, landing gear and tail surfaces as the Lancaster bomber and the prototype flew on 5 July 1942. On 22 April 1944 British Overseas Airways Corporation inaugurated a UK-Cairo route via Morocco, with aircraft diverted from RAF orders. Post-war they were used principally on the UK-Johannesburg Springbok service. British South American Airways was the first company to start regular passenger services across the South Atlantic after the Second World War, flying Yorks to Rio de Janeiro via Lisbon, Dakar and Natal from 15 March 1946.

Curtiss designed the CW-20 as a commercial airliner and the civil prototype NX-19436 flew on 26 March 1940. However, the volumetric capacity of the double-bubble fuselage made it attractive to the US Army Air Corps which ordered it into production in September 1940 as the C-46 Commando. One of many which were civilianised post-war, N10427 was used in Europe by the US cargo carrier Seaboard World Airlines between 1956 and 1970.

After the unflown prototype had been hidden from occupation forces during the Second World War, the prototype Sud Ouest SO-30R Bellatrix flew on 26 February 1945. The production version, the SO-30P Bretagne was used in small numbers in the early 1950s by French colonial operators such as Air Algerie, Air Maroc and Aigle Azur. F-OAIX was fitted with auxiliary Turbomeca Palas jet engines under the wings to evaluate performance improvement for use in Indochina.

Designed for transatlantic operation, the six-engined Latécoère 631 was first flown on 4 November 1942 at Marignane but, seized by the Germans, it was destroyed by Allied aircraft at Friedrichshafen on 17 April 1944. F-BANT was the second airframe, dismantled and hidden during 1944 and flown at Biscarosse on 6 March 1945. Air France accepted three 46-passenger 631s for a Biscarosse-French West Indies route opened in July 1947 but two crashes forced its withdrawal after less than a year.

Development of the Marcel Bloch 161 was continued after the company was nationalised in January 1937 and the prototype flew in September 1939. After the fall of France, twenty were to have been built to German order but the first production SE.161 Languedoc, built by SNCA du Sud-Est at Toulouse, did not fly until 17 September 1945. Having ordered forty of the 33-passenger Languedocs, Air France became the principal airline user; Egypt's Misrair bought SU-AHX from Air France in September 1951.

The British Brabazon Committee's specification 5B for a twin-engined 8-seat light transport, to replace the de Havilland Dragon Rapide, was met by the same manufacturer's D.H.104 Dove, first flown on 25 September 1945. Customers of the 542 built included the Cardiff-based Cambrian Airways, which was merged into BEA on 31 July 1973.

Short Sunderland 3s which had been used by BOAC for wartime services were, with the return of peace, given modified interiors and emerged as the Hythe Class, used to reopen the Empire routes. Sunderland 5s were remodelled as the Sandringham. Export customers included the Norwegian airline DNL which received an initial trio of 37-passenger, radar-equipped Sandringham 6s in 1948 for its Olso-Tromso service.

The opening nose doors of the Bristol 170 Freighter facilitated the quick turnaround required by the cross-Channel car ferry operated by Silver City Airways, initially from Lympne and later from a dedicated terminal at Ferryfield, now known as Lydd. The French destination was Le Touquet, seen below Mk.21 G-AIFV.

Although better known as a civil airliner, the 56-passenger Douglas DC-6 was originally developed for the USAAF as the XC-112. Initial major customers were American Airlines and United Air Lines. Both airlines received first deliveries on 24 November 1946 but United was the first to start coast-to-coast services, beginning on 27 April 1947. XA-JOS was one of three DC-6s delivered to Mexicana in November/December 1950.

BOAC acquired five former USAAF C-69s which were overhauled and delivered between May and July 1946. The airline inaugurated twice-weekly services from London and New York, via Shannon and Gander, on 1 July. BOAC's 1,000th crossing of the North Atlantic was made by G-AHEN on 4 April 1948.

Delays in the delivery to British Overseas Airways Corporation of its ordered Avro Tudors resulted in interim capacity being provided by the civil conversion of twelve Handley Page Halifax C.8s by Short Bros & Harland Ltd. The resulting HP.70 Halton 1, of which G-AHDU was the prototype, could carry ten passengers and 8,000 lb (3,629 kg) of freight in the ventral pannier. They were used for about a year on the London-Accra route and were sold in July 1948.

Plans to build a fleet of seventy-one Avro Tudor 2s for Empire route operation by BOAC, Qantas and South African Airways came to naught with rejection by BOAC in April 1947. Tudor 4 G-AHNJ, here about to depart from London Airport, was, however, one of a number used by British South American Airways for its London-Bermuda route. Two unexplained crashes resulted in the type's withdrawal from use though the surviving aircraft and some stored airframes were later used by Air Charter for trooping and cargo operations.

Miles Aircraft's first all-metal design, the M.60 Marathon was originally to have been used by BEA on its 'highlands and islands' services and by BOAC's associate companies. In fact, 28 of the 40 which were built became RAF navigational trainers in 1953 but 2 of the 6 flown by West African Airways were acquired in October 1955 by Derby Airways, forerunner of British Midland Airways.

Avro Anson military trainers, developed from the Avro 652 used by Imperial Airways on the Croydon-Brindisi route from 1935, became surplus to requirements after hostilities ceased in 1945 and substantial numbers were converted for civilian use, configured with 6-8 seats or as freighters. Transair, based at Croydon, flew up to eleven Ansons on mail and newspaper contracts until Douglas Dakotas replaced then in 1953.

One of the mainstays of British charter companies during the period immediately following the Second World War was the Airspeed Consul, a conversion of the Oxford military trainer with additional windows in the 6-seat passenger cabin and a extended nose for baggage. Over 150 were converted, more than half of them for UK operators. G-AJLR was originally delivered to Olley Air Service at Croydon in June 1947.

The first post-war British transport aircraft to enter airline service, the Vickers Viking, began its regular revenue operations on 1 September 1946 when G-AHOP *Valerie* flew BEA's scheduled service from Northolt to Copenhagen. Det Danske Luftfartselskab, the Danish component of Scandinavian Airline Systems, took delivery of five between April and July 1947, including OY-DLO *Tormund Viking*.

Soviet air transport between the late 1930s and the end of the Second World War was dominated by the PS-84 (Lisunov Li-2) licence-built Douglas DC-3, but in 1946 Ilyushin flew the prototype of the Il-12 which entered service with Aeroflot on 22 August 1947, configured with 21 seats on international services and 27 for domestic use. Small numbers of Il-12s were exported to Czeckoslovakia, Poland and China.

Saab flew the prototype Scandia on 16 November 1946 and began customer deliveries in October 1950. The 24/32-seat unpressurised Scandia began scheduled passenger service on 11 January 1951 over the Oslo-Gothenburg-Copenhagen route of ABA, the Swedish component of Scandinavian Airlines Systems. All seventeen Scandias eventually flew with VASP in Brazil and the last revenue flight was operated on 22 July 1969.

Last of the impressive line of Short flying boats was the S.45 Solent, configured on two decks for up to thirty passengers, with cocktail bar, dining saloon and promenade areas. BOAC inaugurated a Southampton-Johannesburg service on 4 May 1946. Solent G-AHIO *Somerset* finally closed the airline's flying boat operations when it left Southampton on 10 November 1950. Tasman Empire Airways Solent 4 *Aotearoa II* was so named by Princess Elizabeth at Belfast on 26 May 1949.

American Airlines sponsored the development of the pressurised 40-seat Convair 240 which it put into service on 1 June 1948, eventually taking delivery of seventy-five aircraft. Western Airlines, with a fleet of ten, became the second operator, starting services on 1 September. The prototype N24501 had flown at San Diego on 16 March 1947.

Using the wings, engines, tail surfaces and landing gear of the B-29 but with a new 'double-bubble' fuselage seating 89-112 passengers, the Boeing Stratocruiser introduced new standards of space and comfort. Fifty-five were built, Pan American becoming the first revenue operator on 7 September 1948. Northwest Airlines' ten aircraft were the only ones with square cabin windows.

British European Airways bought twenty Airspeed Ambassadors, flying these 40/47-seater short-haul airliners from 13 March 1952 until the latter half of 1957. Pre-production aircraft G-ALFR was experimentally fitted with Napier Eland turboprops in 1955.

The prototype Fiat G.12 made its maiden flight in autumn 1940, this 14-passenger tri-motor having been developed for Avio Linee Italiane. Some G.12s were, instead, built for the Regia Aeronautica as military transports and a small number were completed after the war. These were powered by a variety of engines, including the Pratt & Whitney Twin Wasps installed in the aircraft delivered to Alitalia. I-DALA was the first G.12LP for Alitalia.

Canadair built a Rolls-Royce Merlin engined version of the Douglas C-54 as the DC-4M2 North Star, which also incorporated DC-6 features such as cabin pressurisation, square windows and strengthened landing gear. Trans Canada Air Lines bought twenty, having earlier borrowed six unpressurised DC-4M-1s from the Royal Canadian Air Force to operate the Montreal-London route from 15 April 1947.

Based on a prototype which was flown on 8 May 1943, Savoia Marchetti developed the S.M.95 by lengthening the fuselage by fractionally over 8 ft 3 in, to seat up to twenty-six passengers. Alitalia eventually acquired a total of nine examples and operated the type between April 1948 and 1951.

BOAC was the only original customer for the Handley Page Hermes IV, ordering 25 examples to replace Avro Yorks on its African routes. Configured to carry 40 first-class passengers, the Hermes entered service on the London-Tripoli-Kano-Lagos-Accra route on 6 August 1950. The fleet was sold to a number of British independent operators, including 6 aircraft which Britavia operated from Blackbushe on trooping flights to Cyrpus and Nairobi, beginning in July 1954.

The prototype Breguet Br 761, first flown on 15 February 1959, was known as the Deux Ponts, so called because of its double deck interior layout. The production version was the Br 763 Provence which could accommodate 59 passengers on the upper deck and 48 on the lower; maximum capcity was 135 passengers. Its rear opening doors and ramp facilitated use as a cargo aircraft or vehicle ferry. Air France ordered 12 and a regular service, between Lyons and Algiers, was inaugurated on 16 March 1953.

Intended for transatlantic operation by Air France, the Sud Est SE-2010 *Armagnac* was flown in prototype form on 2 April 1949. Eight production aircraft were built, configured to carry 91-104 passengers, 4 being used by TAI in 1952-53 on pilgrim flights to Jeddah and on a Paris-Morocco service. With 3 others, they were transferred to SAGETA in 1954 and until 1955 were used on flights to Saigon during the war in Indochina. Operations ceased in October 1958.

Bristol-built leviathan – the Brabazon 1 prototype G-AGPW landing at the still camouflaged Filton factory airfield on 6 September 1949, two days later the first flight. Its eight Bristol Centaurus piston engines were to have been replaced by four coupled Proteus turboprops in the 100-seat Mk.II which was designed to fly London-New York non-stop. The latter was never completed and the Mk.1 was broken up in 1953.

A redesign of the Il-12, the Ilyushin Il-14 featured more powerful Shvetsov ASh-82T engines, a new wing and revised vertical tail surfaces, improved radio and instrumentation and thermal de-icing. The 18/26-passenger Il-14P entered Aeroflot service on 30 November 1954 and the stretched IL-14M, the fuselage of which was lengthened by 39 in (1 m) to seat up to 36 passengers, appeared in 1956. Il-14s were also built under licence by VEB in East Germany and, as the Avia 14, in Czechoslovakia.

de Havilland stretched the Dove design into the 14/17-passenger D.H. 114 Heron, the prototype of which flew for the first time on 10 May 1950. BEA used two Heron 1Bs on island services from Glasgow to Barra and Benbecula and to operate Scottish air ambulance flights.

TWA and Eastern Airlines ordered a total of 100 Martin 4-0-4s, the former taking 40 and the latter 60. The 4-0-4 entered service on 5 October 1951 and in January 1952, respectively. The aircraft's predecessor, the unpressurised Martin 2-0-2, had flown slightly earlier than the Convair 240, on 22 November 1946 but structural weakness in the wing brought production to a halt after 31 had been built. The 4-0-4 prototype N40400 flew for the first time on 21 October 1950.

In Britain, British European Airways began to investigate the potential of helicopters for quick inter-city travel in the early 1950s and flew Sikorsky S-51s on a trial service from Northolt to Birmingham's Hay Mills Rotorstation which was inaugurated on 1 June 1951. The operation was replaced by a freight only service from Heathrow to Elmdon Airport, Birmingham on 9 April 1952.

Convair improved the Model 240 by stretching the fuselage to take an extra row of seats, increasing the wing span, thus providing additional fuel capacity in the integral tanks, and by fitting more powerful engines. United Air Lines was the launch customer for the Model 340, ultimately acquiring fifty-five aircraft, but Braniff was the first to operate it commercially, beginning services on 1 November 1952.

The line-up of Lockheed types is dominated by N6202C, the second of 14 L-1049 Super Constellations ordered by Eastern Air Lines. Eastern began Super Constellation service, between Newark and Miami, on 17 December 1951. Behind it is Air France L-749A F-BBDV, one of the final batch of four which brought the French airline's total L-749A purchase to ten aircraft. In the background is the second US Navy XR6O-1 *Constitution*.

Douglas stretched the basic DC-6 by 6 ft 1 in to evolve the 66-passenger DC-6B, 286 of which were built for the world's airlines. United Air Lines inaugurated the first DC-6B transcontinental domestic service on 11 April 1951. Cathay Pacific Airways' VR-HFK, delivered on 9 June 1958, was among the last DC-6Bs to be manufactured.

De Havilland Canada's D.H.C-3 Otter utility transport carried fourteen passengers or one ton of freight and could operate on wheels, skis, floats or as an amphibian. More than 75 per cent of the 466 Otters which were built from 1951 onwards were sold for military use, but the aircraft's STOL performance made it popular with airlines operating from short, unprepared strips, such as Philippine Air Lines. CF-CZO and CF-CZP were used on bush operations by Canadian Pacific Airlines.

Sabena began experimental helicopter operations in 1950 with Bell 47s but introduced the larger Sikorsky S-55 in September 1953 on scheduled internal passenger services, later adding regular flights to Bonn, Eindhoven, Duisburg and Dortmund. They made survey flights to Paris and London.

Perhaps the most aesthetically pleasing derivative of the entire Constellation line was the L-1049 G which, with extra fuel in wingtip tanks, offered improved payload/range performance; ninety-five passengers could be carried. L-1049Gs entered service with Northwest Airlines on 15 February 1955, assigned to the Seattle/Tacoma-Honolulu-Tokyo and Manila route. TWA inaugurated L-1049G services between New York and Los Angeles on 1 April 1955.

Built at Prestwick in the late 1950s, the Scottish Aviation Twin Pioneer demonstrated exceptional short take-off and landing performance and saw extensive military transport use with the Royal Air Force in the Far East and with the Royal Malaysian Air Force. Airline operators of the 16-passenger aircraft included Philippine Airlines, KLM New Guinea subsidiary de Kroonduif, and Borneo Airways.

Further product improvement, including better cabin sound-proofing and an optional 52-seat cabin layout, led to the introduction of the Convair Model 440 Metropolitan, first put into service by Continental Airlines on 8 March 1956. Most were fitted with weather mapping radar in the nose, including OH-LRH which was built for Kar-Air O/Y in January 1958 and sold to Finnair in December 1964.

The Douglas DC-7C was developed in response to a Pan American requirement for a DC-7 with non-stop transatlantic capability both east- and westbound, the latter against the prevailing winds with their adverse effect on range. Extra fuel tankage was provided in the wings which were increased in span by 10 ft (3.05 m). N7DC was the prototype, flown on 20 December 1955 and Pan American put the *Seven Seas* into service on 1 June 1956.

Eight Sikorsky S-58s were purchased by Sabena from the manufacturer and delivered to Brussels between October 1956 and February 1957, their greater capacity and range allowing expansion of the network to include Paris as well as Rotterdam, as seen here. Helicopter operations ceased in October 1966.

Perhaps the ultimate in piston-engined airliners, the Lockheed L-1649A Starliner was given a new, higher aspect ratio wing to accommodate fuel tanks holding 9,600 US gallons and thus gave the aircraft the capability of non-stop operation across the North Atlantic, in both directions. TWA purchased twenty-five and began New York-Paris services on 1 June 1957, followed by Los Angeles-London on 30 September.

Southend-based Air Charter operated vehicle ferries with Bristol Super Freighters and a need to replace them was met by a conversion of the Douglas DC-4. Aviation Traders (Engineering) developed a new forward fuselage with a hinged nose loading door to give access to a 68 ft (20.73 m) long hold; twenty-three passengers were carried in the rear cabin. The first Carvair conversion flew on 21 June 1961 and British United Air Ferries, into which Air Charter had been absorbed, began operations in March 1962.

Numerically the most successful post-war product of the British aerospace industry in the light twin-engined transport category, the Britten-Norman Islander has found acceptance all over the world among operators of bush and outback services. Prototype G-ATCT flew on 13 June 1965, originally powered by Continental IO-360 engines which were soon replaced by Lycoming O-540s.

Four
Brief Glory
for the Turboprop

Turboprop engines promised greater fuel efficiency, reduced cabin noise levels and increased speed – all attractive features to airlines which were still ordering the most advanced piston-engined airliners, principally from the two dominant US West Coast manufacturers Douglas and Lockheed. The diminutive Vickers Viscount, originally specified to have only twenty-four passenger seats, was the first on the scene but it took almost five years for the larger Viscount 701 to achieve in-service status with British European Airways in April 1953; 444 were eventually built, making the aircraft the most successful British civil airliner ever. Vickers later achieved limited success with the Vanguard, and the Hawker Siddeley 748 and Fokker F.27 programmes were also numerically significant.

Bristol flew the elegant Britannia prototype in August 1952 but development problems again delayed entry into service for almost five years and Lockheed's Electra had to undergo structural strengthening of the engine nacelle and adjacent wing structure within little more than a year after it began revenue operations in January 1959.

All of these designs subsequently enjoyed long service lives after sale by their original owners but their first-line careers were relatively short. Pure jet speed and even greater economic advantages were overwhelmingly attractive to longhaul operators and even the short-to-medium range market was being offered jet aircraft as early as May 1955, when Sud-Est flew the prototype Caravelle at Toulouse, the latter being later destined to become the aerospace capital of Europe.

G-AHRF, the prototype Vickers V.630 Viscount, took off on its maiden flight from Wisley on 16 July 1948, piloted by J. Summers and G.R. Bryce. Powered by four Rolls-Royce Dart R.Da.1 engines and seating thirty-two passengers, it was the world's first turboprop airliner and, as part of the certification and development programme, on 29 July 1950 it commenced a month of scheduled operations with British European Airways.

Chief Test Pilot A.J. 'Bill' Pegg flew the prototype Bristol 175 Britannia G-ALBO at Filton on 16 August 1952. Production Britannia 102s entered BOAC service, on the Johannesburg route, on 1 February 1957. Between 9 September and 19 November 1955, G-ANBC was engaged in 250 hours of proving flights in preparation for scheduled service.

Like the Bristol Brabazon, Britain's other great post-war hope for long-range international passenger services, the Saunders Roe S.R. 45 Princess, was destined never to achieve certification. Three examples of the 200-seat flying boat, powered by ten Bristol Proteus turboprop engines, were ordered by the Ministry of Supply for BOAC but only G-ALUN was flown, by test pilot Geoffrey Tyson on 22 August 1952. It and two cocooned aircraft were finally scrapped in 1967.

At one time Europe's most successful short-haul turboprop airliner, the Fokker F.27 Friendship was flown in prototype form on 24 November 1955. Aer Lingus, though not the first to order, became the first to operate the Friendship and EI-AKA was one of two aircraft handed over simultaneously at Amsterdam-Schiphol on 19 November 1958.

For use in and out of lesser airports and unprepared strips, the Antonov An-10 was first flown at Kiev in March 1957. In civil guise it could carry up to eighty-four passengers and entered service with Aeroflot on 22 July 1959, linking Simferopol, Moscow and Kiev. The improved An-10A, stretched by 6 ft 7 in (2.0 m), was a 100-seater and went into service in February 1960.

Developed for Aeroflot's domestic trunk routes, the 90/110-seat Ilyushin Il-18 began passenger services on 20 April 1959. B-208 is an Il-18 of Civil Aviation Administration of China.

A development of the Tu-95 bomber the Tupolev Tu-114 was fast, cruising at a minimum of 466 mph (750 km/h), and endowed with exceptional range. The protoype flew on 15 November 1957 and scheduled service was inaugurated by Aeroflot on 24 April 1961, between Moscow and Kharbarovsk. Tu-114Ds, with auxiliary fuel tanks and seating reduced from a maximum of 224 to 100, began flying the world's longest air route in January 1963. The westbound flight of 6,773 miles (10,900 km) from Havana to Moscow was operated non-stop.

Eastern Air Lines was the first operator of the Lockheed Electra, placing it in service on 12 January 1959 on the New York-Miami route and retaining some as late as 1977 to back up Douglas DC-9s on the Boston-New York-Washington shuttle service. Trans-Australian Airlines' order for a third aircraft was Lockheed's last sale for the Electra.

The ultimate Viscount – the Series V.810 was powered by uprated Rolls-Royce Dart Mk. 525 turboprop engines and was initially developed to meet a Continental Airlines requirement, the Denver-based airline ordering 15 V.812s in December 1955. Continental operated its Viscounts with 52 seats in the main cabin and 4 in the rear lounge and inaugurated service, on its Chicago-Kansas City-Los Angeles route, on 14 February 1958.

Handley Page initially flew the prototype Herald on 25 August 1955 with four Alvis Leonides piston engines but replaced them by two Rolls-Royce Dart turboprops, the aircraft flying in this form on 11 March 1958. The first customer for the stretched Series 200 version, with maximum capacity increased from 44 to 56 seats, was Jersey Airlines which accepted its first aircraft in January 1962 for Channel Islands-UK services.

The twin rotor system favoured by Piasecki Helicopter Corporation, later known as Vertol Aircraft Corporation, was used in the twin-turbine 25-seat Boeing Vertol 107. The prototype flew on 22 April 1962 and New York Airways took delivery of five, using them on its inter-airport passenger services and to the heliport at West 30th Street and the Downtown Heliport near Wall Street.

Armstrong Whitworth's private venture AW650 Argosy had hinged nose and rear doors to give access to the 3,680 cu ft capacity cargo hold. The prototype flew on 8 January 1959 and the first customer was Miami-based Riddle Airlines whose seven Argosy 101s were used on a Military Air Transport Service contract which began on 15 January 1961. G-APRL was the first production Argosy, fitted with clamshell rear doors with an integral loading ramp, to become the aerodynamic prototype for the Royal Air Force's A.W 660 Argosy C.1.

Vickers secured orders from just 2 customers for the 139-passenger Vanguard. British European Airways contracted for 20 and began sustained scheduled service on 1 March 1961. Trans-Canada Air Lines, which became Air Canada on 1 June 1964, beat BEA by a month and introduced the first examples of its 23 Vanguards on 1 February.

To extend the life of piston-engined Convairliners following the introduction of new turboprop designs, a number of conversions were engineered in the mid 1960s with engines which included the Napier Eland, the Rolls-Royce Dart and the Allison 501. The latter was installed in the Convair 580, the most successful of the offered conversions. Allegheny Airlines was a major user and its fleet included forty-four examples.

Designed to replace ageing Lisunov Li-2s and Ilyushin IL-14s, the Antonov An-24 was to be flown on Aeroflot's local service routes, using basic or unprepared airfields. Originally to have capacity for 32-40 passengers, the An 24 was later configured with 44 seats as the An-24V and the An 24 Series II carried 50 passengers. The protoype An-24 flew in April 1960 and production aircraft were introduced on routes from Moscow to Voronezh and Saratov in September 1963.

Avro's Type 748 design study was formally launched by parent Hawker Siddeley Aviation in January 1959 and the first prototype flew on 24 June 1960. Aerolineas Argentinas was the first customer, with an order for nine, and initiated the world's first scheduled 748 services in April 1962. LV-HHC is seen over Buenos Aires on approach to the Aeroparque airport.

Canadair built twelve CL-44-6 Yukons for the Royal Canadian Air Force and developed the CL-44D4 for the civil market. The whole of the latter model's tail section swung aside to facilitate direct loading of bulky cargoes. Initial customer was The Flying Tiger Line which accepted the first of its order for twelve in May 1961.

On 1 March 1962, Los Angeles Airways introduced the world's first multi-engined, turbine-powered passenger helicopter service, using the Sikorsky S-61L. Developed from the S-61A amphibious assault transport, the S-61L protoype flew on 6 December 1960. Although the boat hull was retained it was no longer watertight because of the addition of rear baggage holds; the stabilising sponsons were also removed and fixed landing gear added.

First flown on 7 August 1962, the amphibious 22-passenger Sikorsky S-61N was used by New York Airways to fly visitors to the New York World Fair and on 21 December 1965 the company inaugurated regular service from John F. Kennedy International Airport to the Pan American building in the heart of the city. FAA approval for IFR operation, given on 6 October 1964, was invaluable to operators such as Greenland's Gronlandsfly, flying a network of scheduled services from Godthaab.

Japan's first post-war indigenous transport aircraft, the NAMC YS-11 carried sixty passengers in its initial production version; deliveries to Japan Domestic Airways and Toa Airways began in March and April 1965. Anchorage-based Reeve Aleutian Airways' N173RV was among the last to be built of the total production of 182 aircraft.

Avions Max Holste evolved the M.H.260 feederliner but it was Nord Aviation that was responsible for limited production and for the development of the larger, much redesigned 29-passenger N 262, flown as a prototype on 24 December 1962. US regional carrier Lake Central Airlines bought 8, putting the type into service in mid 1965. Vancouver-based B.C Airlines bought 4 from Allegheny Airlines, with which LCA had merged in July 1968.

A feature of the Shorts Skyvan utility transport was the 6 ft 6 in square hold, 16 ft 6 in long, which was loaded through a full width, upward opening door in the underside of the rear fuselage. Aeralpi took delivery of the first production Skyvan I-TORE in the summer of 1966 for operation from its mountain-surrounded airstrip at Cortina d'Ampezzo.

Lockheed brought the Hercules to the civil market with Model L100 demonstrator N1130E which made a 25 hour 1 minute maiden flight on 20-21 April 1964. Alaska Airlines leased it for a short period, becoming the first civil operator on 8 March 1965.

Although developed for operations from unsophisticated strips exemplified by this landing view of the third de Havilland Canada Twin Otter CF-SUL, the 18-passenger aircraft sold in substantial numbers to third-level and commuter operators throughout the world. Paradoxically, its STOL performance allowed it to fly into major airports with a minimal effect on faster traffic, sometimes using dedicated runways. CF-SUL was delivered to Northern Consolidated Airways, Alaska, as N4901 in February 1967.

Fairchild at Hagerstown, Maryland, built 205 Fokker Friendships under licence. The first US-built F-27 was delivered to West Coast Airlines in July 1958. The stretched Fairchild Hiller FH-227 was flown in January 1966 and customers included Piedmont Airlines.

Beechcraft designed the 17-passenger Beech 99 specifically for US domestic third level and commuter customers, though it sold well elsewhere, particularly in Canada and Europe where there was a similar niche market. The prototype flew in July 1966 and initial deliveries, to Commuter Airlines, began in May 1968. N496HA was originally operated by Henson Airlines, part of the Allegheny Commuter system.

Five
The Turbojet Age Begins

The availability of a practical turbojet engine, in the form of the de Havilland Engine Company's Ghost, gave the airframe arm of the de Havilland organisation the opportunity to steal a march on its rivals, resulting in the first flight of the Comet 1 jet airliner on 27 July 1949. The world's first scheduled jet services were flown by BOAC in May 1952 and it is arguable that de Havilland would have achieved spectacular commercial success had the bold leap forward not been compromised by tragic accidents in 1953 and 1954, which were ultimately attributed to metal fatigue causing failure of the pressure cabin. Even so, the further developed Comet 4 was able to make the first scheduled crossing of the North Atlantic on 4 October 1958, just three weeks before Boeing's first jetliner, the 707-120, could do so with its initial operator Pan American World Airways.

Boeing may have been later on the scene but the 707 was to be the foundation on which the Seattle-based manufacturer built a reputation for cost-effective and reliable airliners. This led to massive order books for all of the company designs which followed it, including the 747 which was the only wide-bodied jetliner to fly within the fifty year period covered in this volume. Douglas and Lockheed, which had been leading the field in the piston era, were overshadowed and the latter, indeed, confined its jet transport interest to military programmes.

The world's first supersonic airliners had flown within twenty years of that first flight by the Comet prototype, led by Russia's Tupolev Tu-144 on 31 December 1958, followed by the Aerospatiale/BAC Concorde on 2 March 1969. The former's technical problems restricted its passenger carrying commercial operational life to less than a year but Concorde survived political pressure to cancel the programme, even though the only customers to confirm their initial interest and commit to firm orders were Air France and BOAC, the state airlines of the two nations that sponsored it. Nevertheless, Concorde will now fly well into the next century, having established niche markets supported by those passengers willing and able to pay surcharged fares for the time-saving advantages of Mach 2 flight.

First flown on 27 July 1949, de Havilland D.H.106 Comet G-5-1 was the first of two prototypes and preceded nine production Comet 1s for BOAC. The world's first jet airliner service with fare-paying passengers was operated by Comet 1 G-ALYP from London to Johannesburg on 2 May 1952. Although a series of tragic accidents, attributed to metal fatigue, caused the type to be grounded in April 1954, it revolutionised passenger travel and cut flying times by over 50 per cent.

Two Comets in BOAC livery, though neither was actually used by the airline commercially. In the background is Comet 2E G-AMXD, used for route proving in 1957-58, prior to the introduction of the Comet 4 which was developed from, in the foreground, the stretched Comet 3 G-ANLO. The latter was first flown on 19 July 1957.

Developed from the Tu-16 bomber, the Tupolev Tu-104 was the world's second jet-powered airliner to achieve in-service status. The prototype flew on 17 June 1955 and caused a sensation when it visited London Airport on 22 March 1956 in connection with the visit of Soviet leaders Bulganin and Kruschev. The initial 50-seat version began domestic service over Aeroflot's Moscow-Irkutsk route on 15 September 1956. Seventy seats were installed in the Tu-104A and, delivery priority being given to CSA, the Czech airline received its first aircraft in November 1957. Aeroflot also used the stretched 100-seat Tu-104B.

Initially known as the Boeing 367-80, the Boeing 707 was developed as a turbojet-powered replacement for the Stratocruiser airliner and the related KC-97 Stratotanker. The protoype flew on 15 July 1954; in October the USAF ordered substantial numbers of KC-135 tankers and on 13 October, Pan American ordered six 707-121s, capable of carrying up to 179 tourist class pasengers. Service across the North Atlantic, from New York to London, began on 26 October 1958. Only Qantas bought the -138 short fuselage version, reduced in length from 144 ft 6 in (44.04 m) to 134 ft 6 in (41.0 m).

This apron scene at Vienna's Schwechat Airport in the early 1960s demonstrates the wide acceptance of the Sud Aviation Caravelle by European airlines, operators including Swissair, Air France, Sabena and Austrian Airlines. The prototype flew on 27 May 1955 and launch customer Air France began revenue operations, with a service from Paris Orly to Istanbul, via Rome and Athens, on 6 May 1959.

Despite the setback of the Comet 1 disasters, de Havilland persevered with development of the Comet 4, nineteen of which were ordered by BOAC in 1957. The first made its maiden flight at Hatfield on 27 April 1958 and, after extensive route proving trials, the first ever transatlantic revenue jet flights were made by Comets G-APDC and G-APDB on 4 October, respectively flying the westbound and eastbound services to London and New York.

Announced in June 1955, the Douglas DC-8 was originally launched as a domestic airliner, attracting initial orders from United Air Lines and Delta Air Lines, with which, as the DC-8-11, it went into service simultaneously on 18 September 1959. Deliveries of the DC-8-32 intercontinental version, for which the launch customer was Pan American, to European carriers KLM, SAS and Swissair began in March and April 1960.

Whereas the Boeing 707-120 was intended for US domestic transcontinental operations, the 707-320 was the larger Intercontinental version, first flown on 11 January 1959 and put into service by Pan American across the North Atlantic on 10 October of that year. Fitted with turbofan engines, the model became the 320B and the passenger/cargo 320C, which proved to be the most popular with the world's airlines, featured a large forward cargo door on the port side. 707-331 N704PA was delivered to Pan American in March 1960.

Though smaller than either the Boeing 707 or the Douglas DC-8, the Convair 880 was faster than both. TWA was the sponsoring airline, ordering thirty, although financing problems led to delivery delays and early aircraft being leased to Northeast Airlines. TWA began services in January 1961. Delta Air Lines, which had contracted for ten aircraft when TWA placed its order, was the first operator, beginning services on 15 May 1960.

In November 1957 Boeing announced a short- to medium-range version of the 707, with a fuselage a little shorter than that of the original 707-100 but a wing of equal span which introduced increased leading edge sweep between the inboard nacelles and the fuselage and almost full-span Krueger leading-edge flaps. United began service on 5 July 1960. Lufthansa's D-ABOH, delivered on 8 March 1961, is of a later 720B version, with Pratt & Whitney JT3D turbofan engines.

With Pratt & Whitney JT3D-1 turbofan engines, the original prototype DC-8-10 became the DC-8-50 and was flown as such on 20 December 1960. Deliveries of Series 50 aircraft, to KLM, began in April 1961. ZK-NZE was accepted by Air New Zealand on 27 February 1968 and was one of the later aircraft, production ending in November 1968.

Although American Airlines was the launch customer for the Convair 990 Coronado, the aircraft's first operator was Swissair, whose route from Zurich to Tokyo was first flown by the type on 9 March 1962. American's CV-990 services were inaugurated on 18 March, between New York and Chicago .

Deriving its name from its 3 Rolls-Royce Spey 505 engined layout, the Hawker Siddeley HS 121 Trident flew for the first time on 9 January 1962. Sponsor airline BEA bought 24 Trident 1s, configured to seat up to 103 passengers, and began revenue services on 1 April 1964. Designed to have an automatic landing capability, the Trident 1 made a first passenger service automatic landing in June 1965. G-ARPE undertook a Far East demonstration tour in autumn 1963 and is seen in Hong Kong.

BOAC's requirement for a replacement for its Comet 4s, used primarily on its African and Far Eastern routes, was met by the Vickers VC-10, first flown in prototype form on 29 June 1962. The 135/152-passenger VC-10 began revenue operations on 29 April 1964, on the London-Lagos service. A small number of the twelve aircraft built for BOAC remained in service briefly after British Airways was formed on 1 April 1974 but five were leased and later sold to Gulf Air to start the airline's route to London.

Trans-Canada Air Lines specified the Rolls-Royce Conway turbofan for its DC-8-43s, Canadian Pacific Airlines and Alitalia being the only other airlines to choose the British engine. TCA became the launch customer for the DC-8F Jet Trader, an all-cargo or convertible passenger/freighter version based on the Series 50 but with a side-loading forward cargo door, reinforced floor and built-in cargo-handling provision. CF-TJL, test flown on 29 October 1962 and used for the certification programme as N9609Z, was delivered on 24 April 1963.

Ilyushin's Il-62 entered cargo service with Aeroflot on 1 March 1967 and started intercontinental passenger services, between Moscow and Montreal, on 15 September. YR-IRA was the first of three Il-62s delivered to Romanian flag carrier Tarom.

Boeing's Model 727 was the first turbine-powered transport to achieve sales in excess of 1,000 examples and was launched on 5 December 1960 when United Air Lines and Eastern Air Lines each ordered forty aircraft. They respectively inaugurated services on 1 and 6 February 1964. Lufthansa was the first non-US customer and it began revenue operations on 16 April. The advanced leading edge slats are clearly seen in this pre-delivery photograph at Renton.

First flown as a prototype on 20 August 1963, the British Aircraft Corporation BAC One-Eleven was launched with an initial order from British United Airways for 10 Series 200s, the second contract being placed by US carrier Braniff International, for 6. BUA began services on 9 April 1965. American Airlines was another major US operator, with 30 Series 401AKs in service from March 1966 until January 1972.

In June 1962 Tupolev embarked upon a radical redesign of the Tu-104, introducing a T-tail and moving the engines to the rear fuselage. The 64/72-seat Tu-134 entered domestic service with Aeroflot in 1966 and was followed by the stretched 80-passenger Tu-134A; export customers included East German flag carrier Interflug.

Delta Air Lines opened scheduled services with the short fuselage 90-passenger Douglas DC-9-14 on 29 November 1965 and TWA, as the second US customer, began to receive its aircraft in February 1966. Production of the DC-9 Series 10 totalled 137 aircraft.

Scandinavian Airline Systems wanted a DC-9 for operation from short runways and Douglas evolved the Series 20, which combined the fuselage of the Series 10 with the long span slatted wing of the Series 30. SE-DBS was the third of ten and was delivered in January 1969 when the airline began regular services.

The first stretch of the basic DC-8 design was applied to the Series 61, the fuselage of which was lengthened by 36 ft 8 in (11.18 m) to increase accommodation to up to 259 passengers. The Series 62 was stretched by just 6 ft 8 in (2.03 m), to carry up to 189 pasengers, but featured an increase in span of 6 ft (1.83 m), additional fuel capacity and drag-reducing aerodynamic refinements.The DC-8-63, prototype N1503U flown on 10 April 1967 and delivered to KLM on 8 November 1967 as PH-DEA, combined the long fuselage of the Series 61 with the improvements incorporated in the Series 62.

Fokker's turbojet successor to the turboprop Friendship, the F.28 Fellowship was flown as a prototype on 9 May 1967 and the initial 65-passenger Mk 1000 production version went into service with Norwegian airline Braathens SAFE on 28 March 1969. The Swedish domestic carrier Linjeflyg was Fokker's biggest single customer for the F.28, taking delivery of twenty aircraft between May 1973 and September 1987.

When Boeing announced the Model 737 in February 1965, the comparable BAC One-Eleven had already flown and the maiden flight of the Douglas DC-9 was imminent – it subsequently proved to be spectacularly more successful than both. The programme began with an order from Lufthansa for twenty-one 100-seat 737-100s, the German company becoming the first non-US airline to be the initial customer for a completely new US airliner. The prototype 737 N73700 flew for the first time on 9 April 1967 and Lufthansa inaugurated revenue services on 10 February 1968.

Although it retained the above-floor fuselage cross-section commonality with the 707, which was a feature of the original 727, the 727-200 was lengthened by 20 ft (6.10 m) to allow maximum passenger capacity to be increased from 131 to 189. Northeast Airlines launched 727-200 operations on 14 December 1967; 1,260 727-200s were built, in addition to 572 -100s.

Douglas also built the stretched 125-seat DC-9 Series 40 to meet a Scandinavian Airlines Systems requirement, although Toa Domestic Airlines of Japan also bought some for similar high-capacity, short-range operations. The prototype N8960U flew on 28 November 1967 and became SE-DBX on delivery to SAS, who inaugurated services on 12 March 1968.

126

Tupolev's Tu-154 was the first Soviet airliner to fly with power-operated controls, prototype SSSR-85000 making its maiden flight on 4 October 1968 at the Zhukovsky test centre. Initially seating up to 158 passengers, the TU-154 began to join the Aeroflot fleet in August 1970 and, following cargo flights which began in July 1971, it was introduced to passenger service on 15 November 1971, from Moscow to Simferopol and Mineralnye Vody.

The world's first supersonic transport to fly was the Tupolev Tu-144 which made its maiden flight on 31 December 1968 and in 1970 achieved Mach 2.4. SSSR-77102 suffered structural failure during an extreme unplanned manoeuvre at the Paris Air Show on 3 June 1973 but the programme continued; regular cargo services between Moscow and Alma Ata began on 26 December 1975. Scheduled passenger services over the same route began on 1 November 1977 but a second crash occurred on 23 May 1978 and services were discontinued on 30 May.

Aerospatiale-assembled pre-production Concorde 02 F-WTSA was essentially to production Series 200 standard, featuring increased fuel capacity, thrust reversers, modified intakes and wing leading edges and a lengthened tail cone. The prototype of the world's first supersonic airliner flew on 2 March 1969 and exceeded Mach 2 in level flight on 4 November 1970. Air France and British Airways were the sole customers and inaugurated services on 21 January 1976, respectively from Paris to Rio de Janeiro and London to Bahrain.

'Jumbo jet' is now a generic term applied by the media to all wide-bodied airliners but the Boeing 747 was the first and represented a quantum leap in size, if not in technology. The first 747-100 flew on 9 February 1969 and Pan American, the launch customer for the aircraft which seated 66 passengers in first class and 308 in tourist class, inaugurated 747 service on the New York-London route on 22 January 1970. Japan Air Lines was the first non-US airline to buy, taking delivery of its first in April 1970.